BORN TO SOAR & DRIBLE: Mark's & Tony's Story of Resilience

By
Purity Muchiri

MAPLE
PUBLISHERS

Born to Soar and Dribble Mark's and Tony's story of Resilience

Author: Purity Muchiri

Copyright © Purity Muchiri (2025)

The right of Purity Muchiri to be identified as author of this work has been asserted by the author in accordance with section 77 and 78 of the Copyright, Designs and Patents Act 1988.

First Published in 2025

ISBN 978-1-83538-588-3 (Paperback)
   978-1-83538-589-0 (Hardback)
   978-1-83538-590-6 (E-Book)

Illustrated by James Murage
Written by Purity Muchiri
Designed & Edited by James Murage
With the help of the White Magic Book Publisher

Published by:
   Maple Publishers
   Fairbourne Drive, Atterbury,
   Milton Keynes,
   MK10 9RG, UK
   www.maplepublishers.com

A CIP catalogue record for this title is available from the British Library.

All rights reserved. No part of this book may be reproduced or translated by any form or by any means, electronic or mechanical, including photocopying, recording or by any information storage and retrieval system without written permission from the author.

To the ones who believe that even the smallest seeds can grow into mighty trees

To my son, for every shared meal, every patched-up shoe and every dream whispered during our goodnight kiss

I Dedicate this Book

To the Hands that held me up

when the road felt steep,

and the laughter that turned

"Not enough" into "just enough"

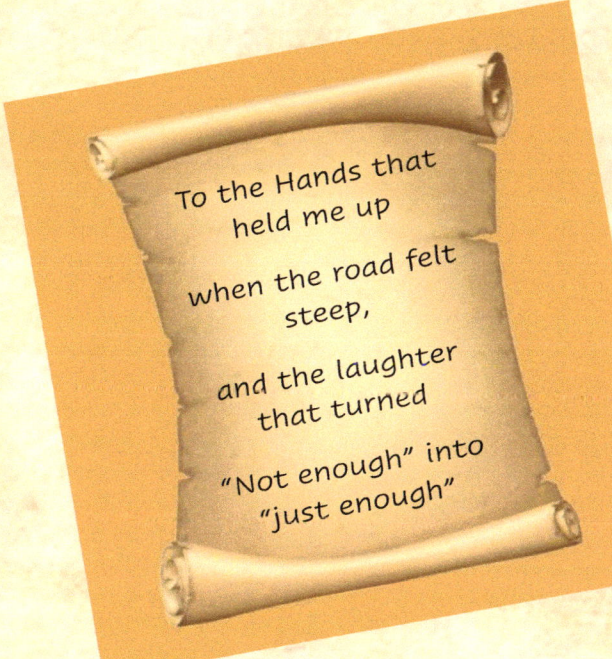

To our Parents who taught us that love outshines gold, and to each other - My brother, my compass, my shelter from the cold.

This story is for every child who dares to begin, because humble roots can grow into big and brave things

AUTHOR'S NOTE

When my son Alexander was born, he was the center of my universe, with sun-kissed skin, beautiful brown eyes, and sweet, gentle cries that could turn me into a human puddle. I've always wanted to hold him in the moment between my first steps, words, and books.

As Alexander grew, as a mother, my fears increased, as I wanted to protect him from the world's cruelties. However, the news of countless humans dying and suffering due to lack of basic needs, made discussing the goodness of this world difficult. He asked tough questions; why are those kids on Tv so thin? Why can't we go feed them? Time had finally caught up with me.

It's then I realized I had to have the big talk with my son. The one where I tell him that, while there are many nice things in the world, problems and challenges also lives with us. And that sometimes people will suffer and you can absolutely do nothing about it. To his surprise, I let him know that the world expected those same people who are disadvantaged to compete with everyone else in all aspects of life.

I wrote *Born to Soar and Dribble* to provide children with a starting point and inspiration about their current situation. This story is for any child who has ever dared to dream big—no matter how small their beginnings are. To every child who dreams of touching the stars or scoring the winning goal: Your story isn't defined by where you start, but by the grit, heart, and joy you carry with you. Keep believing.

I also wrote this book to remind all children, especially those from poor backgrounds, that through hard work, courage, and the unshakable love you can achieve anything. I intended them to learn that teamwork isn't just about passing a ball or sharing a cockpit—it's about lifting each other up, even when the climb feels impossible. JUST DARE TO DREAM.

Mark and Tony were brothers with big dreams. They lived in a simple little home with their dad, a bicycle repairman, and their mom, a tailor.

Mark grew up playing football with a football, homemade with rubber bands and old clothes, practicing on a rough patch of land near their home.

This taught him creativity and adaptability. Although he didn't have fancy equipment, his passion for the game was just enough.

Watching his father repair bicycles with care and precision; Mark learned the value of hard work and patience. Every time he missed a goal, he remembered his father's advice: "If something doesn't work, you don't throw it away; you fix it.

Even though they didn't have much, the small community they lived in supported Mark by showing up for his games and cheering him on, reminding him that success is also about lifting others up.

Tony on the other hand, would sit with his mother as she sewed, watching her turn simple fabric into something new and beautiful. This sparked his imagination, teaching him that even with little, you can create something incredible —just like how he dreamed of transforming himself into a pilot.

While helping his father fix bicycles, Tony learned how every part of a machine works together, which fueled his curiosity about airplanes. He would say, "If I can fix a bike, maybe one day I can fix a plane!" This mindset gave him the confidence to study and understand how things work.

Since flying seemed distant, Tony's love for the sky started with books about planes and stars. He often gazed at the night sky, imagining himself up there, and every plane that flew overhead filled him with determination to turn his dream into reality.

Their parents, despite their humble means, always showed the brothers that with time, dedication, and patience, anything could be achieved.

Their father's skill in fixing things and their mother's ability to craft beautiful garments from simple materials were daily lessons that encouraged both boys to work hard and make the most of what they had.

Mark and Tony grew up knowing the value of gratitude. Even when they began to rise as stars in their respective fields, they never forgot where they came from.

They understood that it wasn't the riches or fame that made them who they were, but their family, community, and the lessons learned from their humble beginnings.

Even after Mark became a football star, he continued to use the principles his father taught him: hard work, fixing mistakes, and appreciating every small victory. He often returned to his hometown to play with the local kids, reminding them that big dreams can start with a simple ball made of rugs.

For Tony, even as a pilot, soaring above the clouds, He never lost sight of the ground he came from. His fascination with how things work, led him to become a pilot and a flight engineer, always curious and learning.

He mentors kids from similar backgrounds, helping them dream of the skies too.

By grounding their success in these lessons from their humble background, the story shows that the greatest stars often shine the brightest when they remember where they came from. Their humble roots gave them the strength and values to rise and succeed, not just in their careers.

ACTIVITY PAGE

Help Tony Color his Jet fighter by using the answers to the Arithmetic problems as the color codes

www.ingramcontent.com/pod-product-compliance
Lightning Source LLC
Chambersburg PA
CBHW042002070526
44584CB00005BA/318